# 101 Things You Need to Know About...

# MUMMIES!

by
## Tim O'Shei

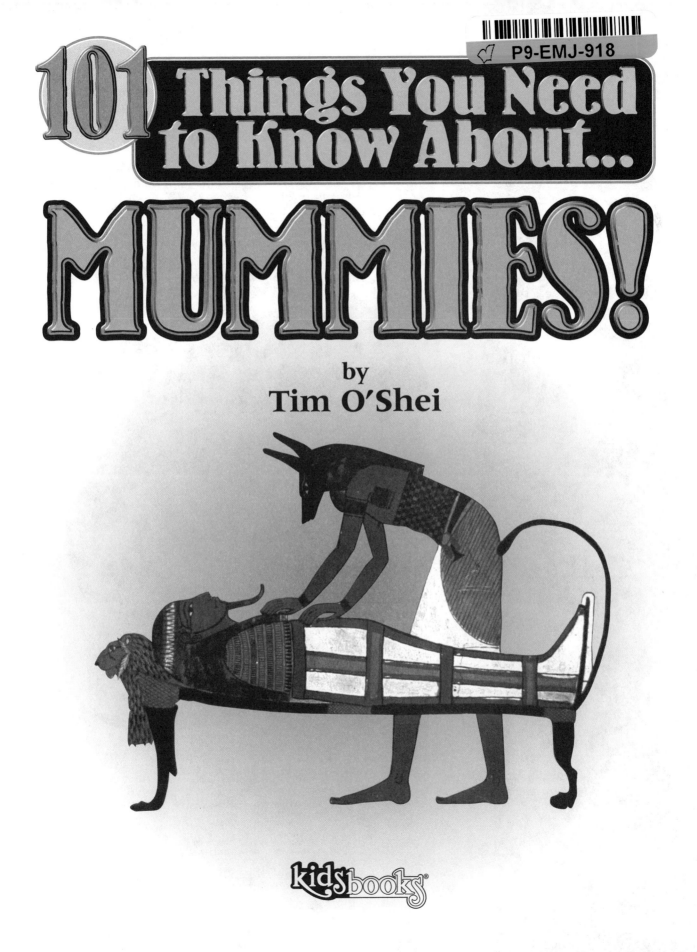

kidsbooks®

## Photo Credits

*Alamy Images:* cover/p. 3
*AP/Wide World:* pp. 4-5, 10, 11, 16, 30, 32, 34, 39, 41, 43, 44, 45
*The Granger Collection:* pp. 6-7, 8-9, 14-15, 17, 23, 25, 26-27, 29, 38
*The Library of Congress Prints and Photographs Division:* pp. 13, 18, 19 (top right; bottom right), 20, 21, 22, 24, 27 (top & bottom), 31, 33 (both), 47, 48
*Greg Reeder:* pp. 12, 19 (top left)

*Visit us at* **www.kidsbooks.com**

# Introduction

You have seen them in books. You have seen them in movies. If you are lucky, you have even seen them up close, in a museum. Everyone has heard about mummies, but how much do you really know about them?

However much mummy knowledge you have stored inside your brain, you're about to learn more. We have collected 101 facts that will:

- tell you how and why the Egyptians made mummies.
- reveal how nature can create mummies.
- describe some of the mysteries and magic surrounding mummies.
- introduce you to some famous mummies, from Egypt's Boy King to Tollund Man.
- give you a taste of mummy medicine, mummy movies, and much, much more.

Pay close attention, because at the end of this book you will find a quiz.

Are you ready to unravel the mysteries of mummies? Let's go!

**golden mask worn by the mummy of Tut, the Boy King of ancient Egypt**

# Who's Your Mummy?

### Here is the skinny

**1.** A **mummy** is a long-dead body that still has some flesh on its bones. That flesh may be skin or internal organs. A mummy is different from a skeleton, which is just the bones of a dead body. Some mummies are so complete, they look as if they are just sleeping. Others have so little flesh left that they are almost skeletons.

### The rap

Here are some terms that you should know:

**2. bacteria:** single-celled microscopic life forms, sometimes known as germs

**3. corpse:** a dead body

**4. decay:** to slowly ruin or fall apart, as when bacteria break down the flesh of a corpse (Usually, over time, a corpse decays until nothing but the skeleton is left. That doesn't happen to a mummified corpse.)

**5. embalming:** the process of treating a corpse so that it will not decay

### To grow or not to grow?

**6.** Bacteria need moisture, warmth, and oxygen to grow. If you take away those conditions, bacteria will grow more slowly—or not at all. A corpse without bacteria at work has a good chance of becoming a mummy.

## Natural or man-made?

**7.** Some corpses become mummies because people have treated the corpses so bacteria cannot grow. This is what the people of ancient Egypt did. (You will learn how later in this book.) Other mummies are formed by accident. Extremely dry heat or freezing cold can turn a corpse into a mummy. Oxygen-free conditions can do that, too, because bacteria need oxygen to survive.

## Far beyond Egypt

**8.** Most people think of mummies as being made only in ancient Egypt. Mummy-making *was* popular there, but Egypt was not the only place it was done. Mummies have been found all around the world. For example, thousands of mummies have been found in South America. They also have been found in Europe, Asia, and other places.

the mummy of Ramses I, king of Egypt from 1292 B.C. to 1290 B.C.

## Mummy chat

**9.** The word *mummy* comes from the Arabic word *mumiyah*, which means "bitumen." Bitumen is a tarlike substance that once was used in the mummifying process.

## The wrap

**10.** Most people think of a mummy as being a corpse that has been wrapped in strips of cloth. That is the most well-known type of mummy, but it isn't the only kind. Many mummies have no wrappings at all.

# A Long Journey

## Life after death

**11.** Why did the ancient Egyptians make mummies? They believed in another life after this one. When the dead person's spirit got there, it would need its body back.

**12.** Turning a corpse into a mummy was the first step toward preparing the dead for the Afterlife. In the Afterlife, people lived in a place called *Amentet*, which meant "the West."

**13.** The Egyptians saw death as a trip across the Nile. A dead person's spirit traveled from the eastern banks of the river to the western side. (The east stood for life, because that is where the sun rises each morning. The west was connected with death, since that is where the sun sets.)

## The trip to Amentet

The Egyptians believed that a person took these steps to reach *Amentet*:

**14.** The newly dead person boarded a boat and sailed through the underworld to the Hall of Truths.

**15.** In the Hall of Truths sat Osiris *(oh-SYE-rus)*, god of the underworld. His job was to decide whether or not the dead person would be allowed to live in *Amentet*. Anubis *(uh-NOO-biss)*, god of mummification, helped Osiris decide.

**16.** Anubis put the dead person's heart on one side of a balancing scale. On the other side was Truth. Osiris did not allow the dead to enter *Amentet* unless his or her heart balanced well against Truth. (That happened only if the person had done more good than bad in life.)

a husband and wife bowing to Osiris

# How to Make a Mummy

## Going natural

**17.** Before the people of ancient Egypt learned how to perform the long, detailed process of mummifying a body, they let nature do the job. They simply buried corpses in the desert sand. This dried and preserved the bodies.

## Ready, set, mummy!

In time, the people of ancient Egypt became master mummy makers. Here is how they did it. (Fair warning: Not all of this is pleasant reading!)

**18.** First, embalmers removed the brain from the skull. They did this by sticking an iron hook in through a nostril and scooping out the brain, piece by piece.

8

**19.** Egyptians believed that the brain served no purpose, which probably is why they got rid of it so rudely. They believed that people think with their hearts.

**20.** Next, they rinsed out the skull. Palm wine and a substance called resin *(REH-zun)* were among the substances used to do this.

**21.** Then embalmers removed most of the body's organs: lungs, stomach, liver, kidneys, and so on. Each was put in its own container, called a **canopic** *(kuh-NOH-pik)* **jar.** (Sometimes, the jars were then placed in a larger container, called a canopic chest.) The heart was left in the body—sometimes wrapped in linen, other times left as it was.

**22.** The embalmers rinsed out the body cavity, then stuffed it to keep its shape. Common stuffings were sawdust or strips of linen. If those were hard to come by, they used desert sand. Sometimes they filled the body with myrrh and spices—even onions, on occasion.

**Anubis preparing a mummy**

**23.** The key to preserving the body was to get it thoroughly dry. The Egyptians did this by covering it in natron *(NAY-tron)*—a saltlike substance—for one or two months. (For common people, this period of time was often much shorter.)

**24.** When the body was dry, it was wrapped in strips of linen that were held in place by resin.

9

**a fully wrapped mummy in its case**

### That's a wrap!

**25.** It could take up to 150 yards of linen strips to wrap a single mummy.

### The line on linen

**26.** Linen is a fabric made from the fibers of the flax plant. Embalmers found linen great for the job because it is lightweight but tough, absorbs moisture, and dries quickly. It also helps keep out bacteria. Linen is a popular fabric today, too, but not for mummy making. We use it in clothing, bedsheets, and tablecloths.

### A weighty subject

**27.** It could take up to 600 pounds of natron to properly mummify one person.

### The jackal-headed god

**28.** Remember Anubis? In Egyptian myths, he is the son of Osiris. When Osiris is killed by his brother, Seth, Anubis invents mummification to preserve the body. Then Anubis leads his father's spirit to the underworld.

**29.** Besides being the god of mummifi-cation, Anubis leads the spirits of the dead to stand before Osiris in the Hall of Truths. He also guards the tombs of the dead.

the mummified body of Harwa, who was about 30 when he died—around 3,500 years ago

## Home, sweet home

**30.** In ancient Egypt, mummifying a corpse was only step one. Next came creating someplace to put it. The people of ancient Egypt went all out—especially for their royalty, who got the finest coffins.

## Pretty as a picture

**31.** At first—back around 2650 B.C. to 2575 B.C.—Egyptians would make a large box for each mummy. One such coffin is called a **sarcophagus** *(sar-KAH-fuh-gus)*. More than one are **sarcophagi** *(sar-KAH-fuh-guy)*. Early sarcophagi were large boxes made of stone. People often decorated them with pictures that looked like doors and windows. (After all, they wanted the mummies to feel at home!)

**32.** Later, Egyptians began making mummy cases out of wood or clay, or metal (even silver or gold). The shapes became less boxy, and more like the bodies inside.

**33.** Body-shaped sarcophagi often had faces painted or carved on them. *(See the photo at left.)* Some were dressed in fine clothes, or decorated with precious jewelry or beautiful pictures.

**34.** Mummies of well-to-do people had masks placed over their faces. A king—called the **pharaoh** *(FAY-roh)*—got gold. Mummies who had been rich, but not royal, got masks made of silver, wood, or plaster.

## The royal treatment

**35.** Around 1539 B.C., Egyptians began to really pile it on. The grander the person, the more coffins he or she got. King Tut (who you will meet later) was the grandest ever found. His mask was made of jewel-encrusted gold, and the body was decorated with jewels and precious charms. Then the mummy was placed in three Tut-shaped coffins, each inside another. First, one of solid gold, then two made of wood that was decorated with gold.

*left:* **the head section of a body-shaped sarcophagus**
*right:* **decorated sarcophagi**

# Stuffed Animals

## Animals prepared for the Afterlife

**36.** Mummification was not only for humans. The people of ancient Egypt—and of other cultures—mummified animals, too. In Egypt, some of the animals, such as gazelles, had been beloved pets. Others, such as cats, were worshipped as gods or goddesses. The Egyptians also mummified animals to serve as food for mummified people in the Afterlife.

## No lying, it's a lion!

**37.** From ancient drawings, archaeologists knew that the Egyptians worshipped lions. Archaeologists long believed that lions were buried in the same tombs as humans, but had no proof. In 2001, they finally got it. The remains of a mummified lion were found in the tomb of Maia *(MY-uh)*, a nurse to King Tut.

## Croco-mummies

**38.** Just over 2,000 years ago, some Egyptians worshipped a crocodile god named Sebek. In his honor, they built a place called Crocodilopolis *(KRAH-kuh-duh-LAH-puh-liss)*, near what today is the town of Al Fayyum. There, Sebek's followers gave crocs the royal treatment. They fed the crocs special food, and adorned them with fine jewelry. Not surprisingly, crocs that died were mummified.

## Hanging around

**39.** Mummifying animals is not just ancient history. A process known as taxidermy *(TAK-suh-dur-mee)* is still practiced today. Taxidermy is a way of preserving an animal's head, or head and body, so that it looks as lifelike as possible. Before zoos became common, stuffing and displaying animals this way helped people learn about creatures that they would never be able to see in the wild. Sometimes, animals are stuffed and hung on walls as hunters' trophies. Mammals and birds are the most popular taxidermy subjects, but reptiles and fish are also done.

Egyptian cat and dog mummies, from about the 1st century A.D.

learning about a 2,500-year-old mummy

## Breaking the code

**40. Hieroglyphics** (*HI-ruh-glih-fiks*) is a system of writing using pictures and symbols instead of letters. For 1,300 years, nobody knew how to read the hieroglyphics written all over many mummies' tombs and sarcophagi. Then, in 1799, French soldiers found an unusual stone near Alexandria, Egypt. Known as the Rosetta Stone, it was carved with a message written in two different kinds of hieroglyphics. The same message was carved in Greek. Experts who knew Greek were able to translate the hieroglyphics on the stone.

## Who was who?

**41.** Decoding the hieroglyphics unlocked many other mysteries. For instance, the names of mummified pharaohs were written on the front of their linen wrappings. This proved very helpful to archaeologists who were trying to identify the remains. Other writings in the tombs described the people and their way of life.

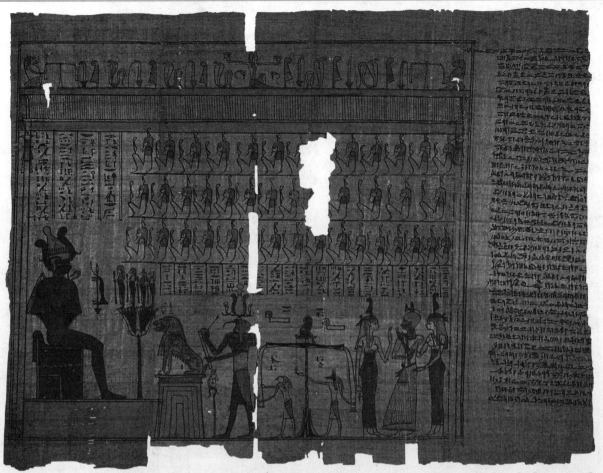

**pages from the ancient Egyptian Book of the Dead**

## Was reading dead?

**42.** Found inside the coffins or tombs of many pharaohs and their family members was something called the Book of the Dead. It was a collection of spells for protecting the mummies, and advice to help them live well in the Afterlife. (The Egyptians called the book *The Chapters of Coming-Forth-by-Day*. The name *Book of the Dead* came from an Egyptologist named Karl Richard Lepsius. He was the first person to publish a version of the book, in 1842.

## Good-bye and good luck!

**43.** The oldest known hieroglyphics are the Pyramid Texts. These were written on the walls inside some of the pyramid tombs at Saqqara *(suh-KAH-ruh)*, Egypt. Like the Book of the Dead, they were prayers and spells meant to protect the mummy on its journey to the Afterlife.

# Welcome to Mummyland!

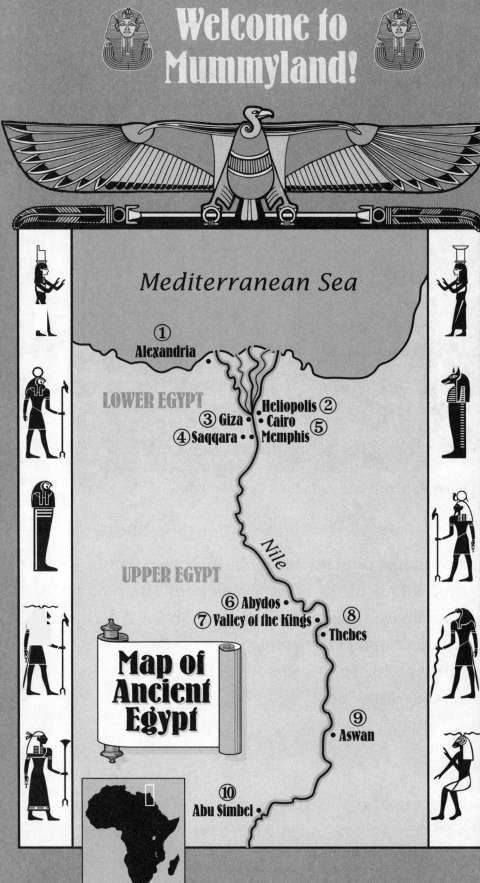

## Map of Ancient Egypt

Mediterranean Sea

① Alexandria

LOWER EGYPT

Heliopolis ②
③ Giza • • Cairo
④ Saqqara • • Memphis
⑤

*Nile*

UPPER EGYPT

⑥ Abydos •
⑦ Valley of the Kings •
⑧ • Thebes

⑨ • Aswan

⑩ Abu Simbel •

① Built by Alexander the Great, Alexandria was one of Egypt's ancient capitals.

② Heliopolis was the center for the worship of Re *(RAH)*, the sun god.

### ③ Giza

**44.** Three pyramids stand at Giza. The largest and most famous is the Great Pyramid, built as a tomb for the pharaoh Khufu (also known as Cheops). The pharaoh Khafre, Khufu's son, has another of the three as his tomb. Nearby, Khafre built a huge sculpture, the world-famous Great Sphinx *(below)*. It has a man's head and a lion's body.

③

### ④ Saqqara

**45.** The first pharaoh to build a pyramid for his tomb was Djoser (or Zoser). Known as the Step Pyramid, it was built at Saqqara, near Djoser's capital, Memphis.

⑤ **Memphis was Egypt's capital from about 2575 B.C. to 2130 B.C. Many ancient cemeteries lie in the area. Cairo is Egypt's capital today.**

### ⑥ Abydos

**46.** This was the center for the worship of Osiris, god of the underworld. The oldest known religious figures of Osiris show him as a mummy with his arms crossed on his chest.

### ⑦ Valley of the Kings

**47.** From about 1539 B.C. to 1075 B.C., royal tombs were built here, including that of the world's most famous mummy, King Tut.

### ⑧ Thebes

**48.** Many kings and queens were buried in tombs carved deep into the rock here. Royals were not the only ones laid to rest at Thebes. Priests, soldiers, and loyal servants were buried in a "city of the dead" here. Today, the ruins of Thebes are known as Karnak and Luxor.

⑨ **Stone for many of Egypt's pyramids, temples, and monuments came from quarries at Aswan.**

### ⑩ Abu Simbel

**49.** Ramses II (whose mummy you can see on pages 22-23), built two temples here. The huge structures were carved into the cliffs that tower over the river.

## Stone collectors

**50.** Death was such a big deal that pharaohs spent most of their lives preparing for it. It was not unusual for a pharaoh to find an entire **quarry** (a place where large amounts of stone are dug out of the ground) and reserve it for the construction of his pyramid.

## Lost and found

**51.** At least 80 royal pyramids have been found in Egypt. Many more may still lie buried under the sands of centuries. Most of the known pyramids were looted long ago. The mummies were taken or destroyed, along with any treasures that may have been put in tombs with them.

**the Great Pyramid, in a photo from about 1934-1939**

tourists climbing the Great Pyramid in 1896

## The incredible shrinking pyramid

**52.** The Great Pyramid at Giza is the largest, grandest mummy mansion of them all. Khufu's mummy and all its treasures disappeared long ago, but the structure built in his honor still stands tall. Not as tall as it once did, though. The Grand Pyramid's original height was 481 feet. Now it is only about 451 feet. At one time, a thick limestone coating gave the pyramid a gleaming white, smooth surface. Over many years, people stripped off the limestone. Millennia of weather also whittled away some of the height. Each side of the pyramid's square base is a little more than 755 feet long—about the length of two football fields.

## How great is great?

**53.** The pyramids at Giza are counted among the Seven Wonders of the Ancient World. In 1979, UNESCO *(yoo-NESS-koh)* named Giza's pyramids—along with Saqqara and three other pyramid sites in the Memphis area—a World Heritage Site, to protect them for the ages. *(UNESCO* is short for the United Nations Educational, Scientific, and Cultural Organization.)

# Cops
# and
# Robbers

the mummy of Ramses II,
one of the pharaohs of
the New Kingdom

## The mummy patrol

**54.** Antiquities *(an-TIH-kwuh-teez)* are items from ancient times. They can be as small as a coin or as large as a pyramid. Over many centuries, Egypt's antiquities had been disappearing at an alarming rate. To keep them safe, Egypt's government founded the Egyptian Antiquities Service in 1835.

## "Not so fast, buddy!"

**55.** On September 10, 1996, a man hid overnight in Cairo's Egyptian Museum. He stuffed his pockets and socks with as many of King Tut's treasures as they would hold. He hid more in a bathroom, to take later. Then he hid again. In the morning, he tried to leave, telling guards that he was a plumber who had been doing some repairs. The guards didn't believe him. They found the loot and foiled the crime.

## Hide-and-seek

**56.** Evil curses were inscribed on the outside of tombs to scare away grave robbers. They didn't work. Even in the time of the pharaohs, the robbing of mummies' tombs was a serious problem. During the New Kingdom (about 1540 B.C. to 1075 B.C.), the pharaohs started building their tombs deep underground in a secret, faraway place. That place, the Valley of the Kings, didn't stay secret for long. People found and broke into most of the hidden tombs soon after they were built. Some of what was found disappeared forever. Some ended up in museums or private collections. Only one royal tomb stayed hidden for many centuries more: the tomb of King Tut.

the mummy's head: Ramses II

**57.** Today, he is the world's most famous mummy. In his day, though, Tutankhamen *(too-tang-KAH-mun)* was not one of Egypt's great rulers. Known as "the boy king," he had the job for only a few years, and was just 18 when he died. What Tut is known for today is his treasure-filled tomb.

*below:* the entrance to King Tut's tomb
*opposite:* Howard Carter *(left)* and an assistant at the mummy's door

## Mum's the word!

**58.** The mummy's tomb was not easy to find. Archaeologists knew about Tut, but his tomb was not one of the many already found. Where was it? Many archaeologists and treasure hunters looked for many years, but no one found it—until Howard Carter. On November 4, 1922, after years of searching the Valley of the Kings, Carter got a huge thrill. Workers had found a flight of stairs, leading down. A few days later, they found a door. Its ancient label and seals were unbroken!

## Worth the wait

**59.** Lord Carnarvon, a rich Englishman, had been covering the costs of Carter's search. Carter waited for Carnarvon to arrive from England. When he arrived, on November 23, the men started chipping their way into the tomb. Several days later, they were in! Carter went in first and met an amazing sight: a room crammed with treasures fit for a king.

## Tut's treasures

**60.** Among the items found in the mummy's tomb were gold vases, jewelry, weapons such as bows and arrows, boomerangs, and a snake-catching stick. There were several oars, too—for the boat that was to carry the king to the underworld.

## Taking it easy

**61.** Everything that a king would need for an easy Afterlife was put in the tomb: baskets, pots, food, toys, weapons, and many other items. A king would not serve himself, so clay models of servants were included, too.

## "Open that door!"

**62.** Tut's mummy—not found till months later—was in a hidden chamber, behind another sealed door. Outside the door stood two life-size statues of the king wearing his royal headdress.

## A mummy's curse?

**63.** Shortly after the discovery of Tut's tomb, people began to wonder if the curses written to protect the mummy were real. Lord Carnarvon, who had been bitten on the face by a mosquito, cut the bite while shaving. Soon afterward, he died of an infection. Carnarvon was not the only one: A Frenchman and an American both died after visiting Tut's tomb. An X-ray specialist who was to examine Tut's body died on his way there. But Howard Carter lived on and did well: He spent the next decade organizing the treasures, and seeing them safely to the Egyptian Museum in Cairo.

Tut in his golden coffin

statue of Tut from his tomb

Tut's canopic chest

27

### For peat's sake!

**64.** A bog is a lowland area that holds water, making the soil like a wet sponge. As moss and other plants die and decompose in a bog area, they form a substance called peat. People have found peat quite useful, because it can be used as fuel for fires. Peat isn't the only thing that bogs are good for. Bogs also are perfect for naturally mummifying dead bodies.

### No air down there

**65.** Wait! The Egyptians created mummies by *drying* bodies, right? How can someplace as damp as a bog do the same job? Here is how: A bog's dense soil has very little oxygen in it. Bacteria need oxygen to grow. No oxygen, no bacteria. No bacteria, very little decomposition.

### Unhappy endings?

**66.** Bodies have been found in bogs throughout Europe, but mostly in Scandinavia. Testing has shown that many of them are well over 1,000 years old. Some bog mummies show signs of violence, leading scientists to think that they were killed, then dumped in the bogs. Some may have been sacrificed as part of ancient religious ceremonies.

### The face looks familiar . . .

**67.** Over time, the bodies sank below the bogs' surface and were mummified by the oxygen-free surroundings. Some of them are amazingly well-preserved. Their features are so clear that they look as if they died quite recently. Bog mummies have red hair and dark-brown skin, the colors caused by acid created by the peat.

## Man of iron

**68.** Perhaps the most famous bog mummy is known as Tollund Man. (He was named for the village near where he was found: Tollund, in Denmark.) Tests show the body to be from about 350 B.C.—early in the Iron Age. Tollund Man is in remarkably good shape. We even know (by the stubble on his face), when he last shaved: two or three days before he died. His new home, Denmark's Silkeborg Museum, has another famous bog mummy, called Elling Woman.

## A very long-lost cousin?

**69.** Some bog mummies have fingerprints that are still intact. Fingerprinting experts have studied them and found the patterns to be similar to those of modern humans.

When two farmers found Tollund Man, in 1950, they called the police. He was so well-preserved, they thought that he might have been the victim of a recent crime.

# Mummies of the Americas

### Across two continents

70. Many Amerindian peoples (Indians of North or South America) made mummies. Mummies have been found from northernmost Canada to the Andes of Peru.

### American idol

71. The most well-known mummies of the Americas were made by the Inca. From the 12th century until 1532, the Inca ruled a vast empire that spread across parts of present-day Bolivia, Chile, Ecuador, and Peru. Hundreds of years ago, they worshipped a mummy of their dead king, who they believed to be a god.

**mummy bundle of an adult and child found in Peru**

### Gifts to the gods

72. When the Inca needed help, they offered their gods a human sacrifice—a person who was killed and mummified as a favor to the gods. The Inca hoped that the gods would return the favor—such as rain to help crops grow.

### An amazing find

73. In 2002, archaeologists uncovered a massive grave site outside the city of Lima, Peru. There, they found the mummified bodies of more than 2,000 Incas. Desert dryness had helped preserve them for about 500 years.

**74.** Some of the Incan mummies were found wrapped in bundles of up to seven bodies each. Archaeologists think that each bundle may have been a family. Some of the mummy bundles were topped with *falsas cabezas* (Spanish for "fake heads").

**75.** The Incan mummies had been buried with thousands of things that they might need in the next life, such as food, cooking utensils, and favorite possessions.

## Unexpected neighbors

**76.** You never know where you might find a mummy. A Georgia farmer named L. J. Gregory found two buried in his yard! They may have been Toltec Indians. In the 10th to 12th centuries, the Toltec ruled the area that is now central Mexico. They lived in other areas, too—including parts of what is now Georgia.

**two Peruvian mummies found in the late 19th century**

## Keep up the good work!

**77.** Like the Egyptians of long ago, the Aleut people of western Alaska removed a corpse's inner organs and washed out the body cavity. Then they dried and wrapped the corpse. They placed the mummy so it was sitting upright. Sometimes, it was set up as if it were at work: a man fishing, for instance, or a woman sewing. Usually, the Aleut mummified only people who had been respected or important in some way. The Kadiak-Inuit of Canada made mummies much the same way as the Aleut, but gave mummy honors only to a special few: men who had been whalers.

## Frozen stiff

**78.** A mummy known as Juanita, the Ice Princess, was found on a Peruvian mountain in 1995. She is the first frozen Incan mummy ever found. A young woman when she died, Juanita is now at least 500 years old.

## Man of the mine

**79.** Some American mummies were the accidental kind—the Copper Man of Chile, for instance. Around the year A.D. 800, a man was working in a copper mine in the Chilean desert. The tunnel collapsed, trapping him inside. The man died, but his corpse was preserved: It was mummified by the combination of dry air and salt inside the mine.

the Ice
Princess
of Peru

## High and dry

**80.** The Kwakiutl *(kwah-kee-YOO-tul)* of British Columbia, Canada, made mummies. The photo below, from early in the 20th century, shows a Kwakiutl man using the smoke of a fire to dry and preserve a corpse being mummified.

**Kwakiutl man and mummy**

# Mummies on Ice

## Discovery on a mountain

**81.** In September 1991, a corpse was discovered in the Ötztal area of the Italian Alps. At first, people thought it was the body of a hiker who had been caught in a snowstorm and died. Scientific tests proved otherwise: It was 5,200 years old! It had been in a deep freeze for thousands of years, until warmer temperatures melted the ice and brought the mummy to light.

Oetzi being examined

**82.** Scientists named the mummy Ötzi—often spelled Oetzi—after the area where he was found. Often, though, he is referred to simply as "the Iceman." Mummification by ice has one serious problem: As soon as the mummy begins to thaw, decay gets started. Scientists rushed Oetzi to a nice, cold lab to preserve and study him.

## Getting acquainted

**83.** Using carbon dating, DNA testing, and other modern high tech, researchers can learn a lot about a mummy's life. For example, we know that Oetzi was in his 30s or early 40s when he died. An arrowhead in his back shows what probably killed him. (Was it a hunting accident—or murder?) Oetzi's last meal was cereal and deer meat.

## Visitors welcome

**84.** Oetzi now has a home: A museum was built, just for him, in Bolzano, Italy. If you are ever in the neighborhood, do drop by!

## An ice-cold trio

**85.** Oetzi is not the only well-known ice mummy. In 1984, researchers on a Canadian island north of the Arctic Circle found three coffins below the frozen surface. The people inside were in perfect shape—for dead men. It was too cold for decay to have set in. These ice mummies turned out to be explorers named William Braine, John Hartnell, and John Torrington. They had been part of Sir John Franklin's 1845 expedition, whose members all disappeared while searching for a Northwest Passage from the Atlantic to the Pacific.

**Quite a crowd!**

**86.** If you take a trip to the Italian island of Sicily, you can visit nearly 6,000 mummies. They are stored in the **catacombs** (a series of tombs in underground chambers). The oldest of the mummies are more than 400 years old; the youngest, a bit more than 70.

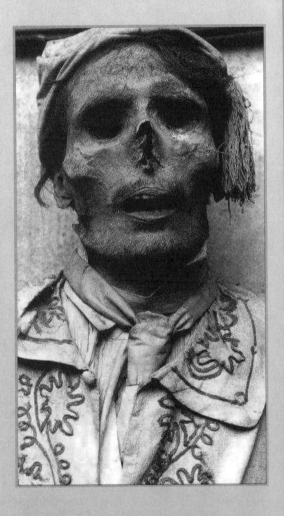

### Worn around the house

**87.** Unlike Egyptian mummies, these bodies were not wrapped in linen. They are dressed in their normal clothes. Only the skin—or bones—of their heads and hands is exposed.

### Paying their respects

**88.** Family members of the deceased would often go to the catacombs to visit and pray for the mummies, just as people do at graves in cemeteries.

### They go back a long way

**89.** The Sicilian mummifications were performed by Catholic monks, who still care for the catacombs today. Many of the Sicilian mummies are priests and monks who came before them.

### A little girl forever

**90.** One of the most famous mummies in Sicily is of a small child. Rosalie Lombardo was only two years old when she died. That was in 1920, but she looks the same now as she did then—right down to the bow in her hair. How was that amazing feat of mummification done? It remains a mystery: No one knows what chemicals were used in the process.

# Mummies Go Global

## Mummies, mummies, everywhere

**91.** Mummies—both embalmed and natural—have been found all over the world. You have already read here about mummies of Egypt, Scandinavia, the Americas, the Arctic, and Sicily. They have been found in the Middle East, the South Pacific, and western China, as well.

## Not just another pretty face

**92.** The Maori people of New Zealand are known for their tradition of intricate tattoos. They once had another tradition, too, of mummifying heads. The skin and hair of these preserved heads is remarkably lifelike—including the tattoos.

the mummified head of a Maori chief

### From out of the west

**93.** The vast Takla Makan Desert, one of the largest sandy deserts on Earth, is not a place many people choose to visit. It is no wonder, then, that no one found its mummies until the late 20th century. The western China mummies are estimated to be 2,000 to 3,000 years old. The colorful clothes were as well-preserved as the people in them.

a baby mummy from about 800 B.C., found in western China

# A Never-ending Tale

If you think that experts now know everything there is to know about mummies, think again!

## What is that glow?

**94.** In 1999, archaeologists unearthed a spectacular find: an ancient cemetery. The hundreds of tombs found at Egypt's Bahariya Oasis hold thousands of mummies. Some of the mummies there had been rich, others poor. The first mummies found there had gold-painted coffins or golden death masks. That is why the area is now known as the Valley of the Golden Mummies. The Bahariya discovery will keep archaeologists, historians, and scientists busy for decades. Besides the mummies and their treasures, researchers have found a wealth of new knowledge. Wall paintings, carvings, and hieroglyphics found in many of the tombs have much to tell us about life thousands of years in the past.

## Aha!

**95.** Did the people of ancient Egypt make human sacrifices? Some archaeologists believed so, but had no proof. In 2004, however, archaeologists announced a major discovery at a king's tomb at Saqqara. Aha, who lived about 5,000 years ago, was one of ancient Egypt's first pharaohs. Close to where his mummy was buried, archaeologists found the skeletons of servants and court officials. All died around the same time as Aha. Had they been sacrificed to serve the king in the Afterlife? That seems to be the case!

### Take one mummy and call me in the morning

**96.** Back in the Middle Ages, mummy powder was the latest in medical know-how. The popular medicine was just what it sounds like: a mummy's wrappings—or the mummy itself—pounded into a powder. (That is one reason why Egypt has more mummy tombs than mummies.) By the way, there is no proof that mummy powder cured anybody.

### Dating mummies

**97.** Even mummies found long ago may have new stories to tell us. As fast as technology comes up with new tools to use, scientists have found ways to use them for studying mummies. Take carbon dating, for instance. It was developed in the 1940s as a way to measure rates of decay. Mummy researchers immediately adopted it as a way to figure out the age of mummies and the objects found with them.

### "Arrest that mummy!"

**98.** Many of the scientific techniques that the police use to solve crimes have helped solve mummy mysteries as well. Fingerprinting, DNA testing, skin and bone analysis, and many other lab tests are a few of the many crime-fighting tools that have come in handy, mummywise. Finding out how, when, where, and why a mummy died—and how it was preserved—tells us a lot about that person's culture, environment, and period in history.

### Sneak peeks

**99.** X rays and CT scans (also called CAT scans) allow researchers to see inside a mummy's body. When something has lasted thousands of years, why cut it open if you don't have to?

CT scan for a mummy
found in Arizona's
Gila Bend Desert
in 1895

43

# Fun With Mummies

## Larger than life

**100.** Mummies have long been a subject of horror flicks and thrillers. *The Mummy*, made in 1932, is one of the earliest mummy movies. Boris Karloff became famous as the man in rags. His costume, by the way, was loosely based on the real mummy of King Ramses III. Two of the most popular mummy movies ever are recent ones. Perhaps you have seen them: *The Mummy* (1999) and its sequel, *The Mummy Returns* (2001).

a wax figure of Boris Karloff in his most famous role

# The Last Word

## Get wrapped up in history!

**101.** Mummies can be spooky, scary, and sometimes creepy, but they are always fascinating. If you ever get a chance to see a real one for yourself, do it! Many museums have human or animal mummies, including the American Museum of Natural History in New York, the Denver Museum of Nature and Science, the Field Museum in Chicago, and the Smithsonian Institution in Washington, D.C. The British Museum in London, England, has a big collection of mummies. You can see bog mummies in Scandinavia, Incan mummies in South America, and Egyptian mummies in (where else?) Egypt.

**checking out the mummy of Ta-bes, who lived sometime around the 5th century B.C.**

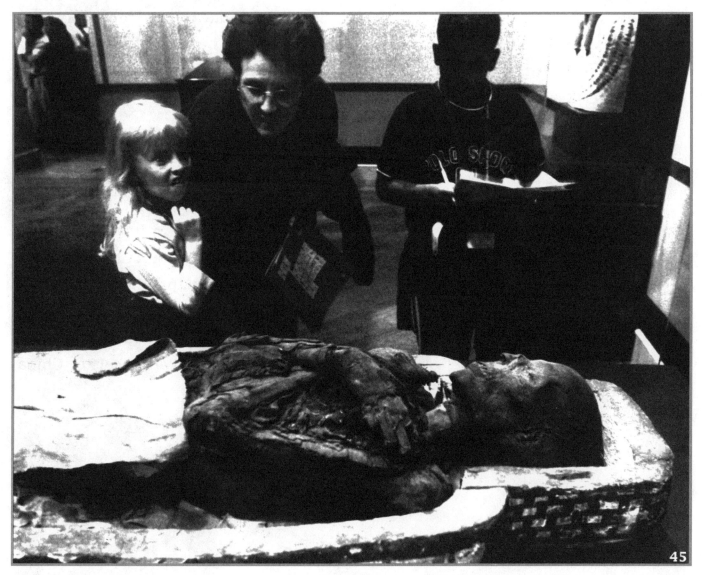

1. Which of the following is *not* an environment in which a "natural" mummy can be made?
   a. extremely cold temperatures
   b. a hot and humid environment
   c. an oxygen-free environment
   d. very dry heat

2. Which of these is a word for the process of treating a corpse so that it will not decay?
   a. bacteria
   b. bitumen
   c. embalming
   d. *mumiyah*

3. What is the name of the saltlike substance that ancient Egyptians used to dry out bodies?
   a. limestone
   b. myrrh
   c. natron
   d. palm wine

4. Which organ of the body did the ancient Egyptians think served no purpose?
   a. brain
   b. heart
   c. kidneys
   d. lungs

5. Which pharaoh is known as the Boy King because he was only 18 when he died?
   a. Aha
   b. Djoser
   c. Ramses II
   d. Tutankhamen

6. Oetzi the Iceman became mummified after an accident where?
   a. the Italian Alps
   b. a mine in Chile
   c. a peat bog in Scandinavia
   d. the Takla Makan Desert of China

7. **What are *falsas cabezas*?**
   a. fake heads found on some Incan mummy bundles
   b. a name for the bog mummies of Denmark
   c. possessions put inside a pharaoh's tomb
   d. prayers in the Book of the Dead

**Which of the following are you likely to see on mummies made by the Maori of New Zealand?**
   a. colorful clothing
   b. linen wrappings
   c. red hair
   d. tattoos

9. **Which of the following allows researchers to see inside a mummy's body?**
   a. carbon dating
   b. CT scans
   c. DNA tests
   d. mummy powder

10. **Where are the mummies of Sicily stored?**
   a. in bogs
   b. in catacombs
   c. in pyramids
   d. in sarcophagi

**Amenhotep II, who ruled Egypt in the 15th century B.C., in his royal tomb at Thebes**

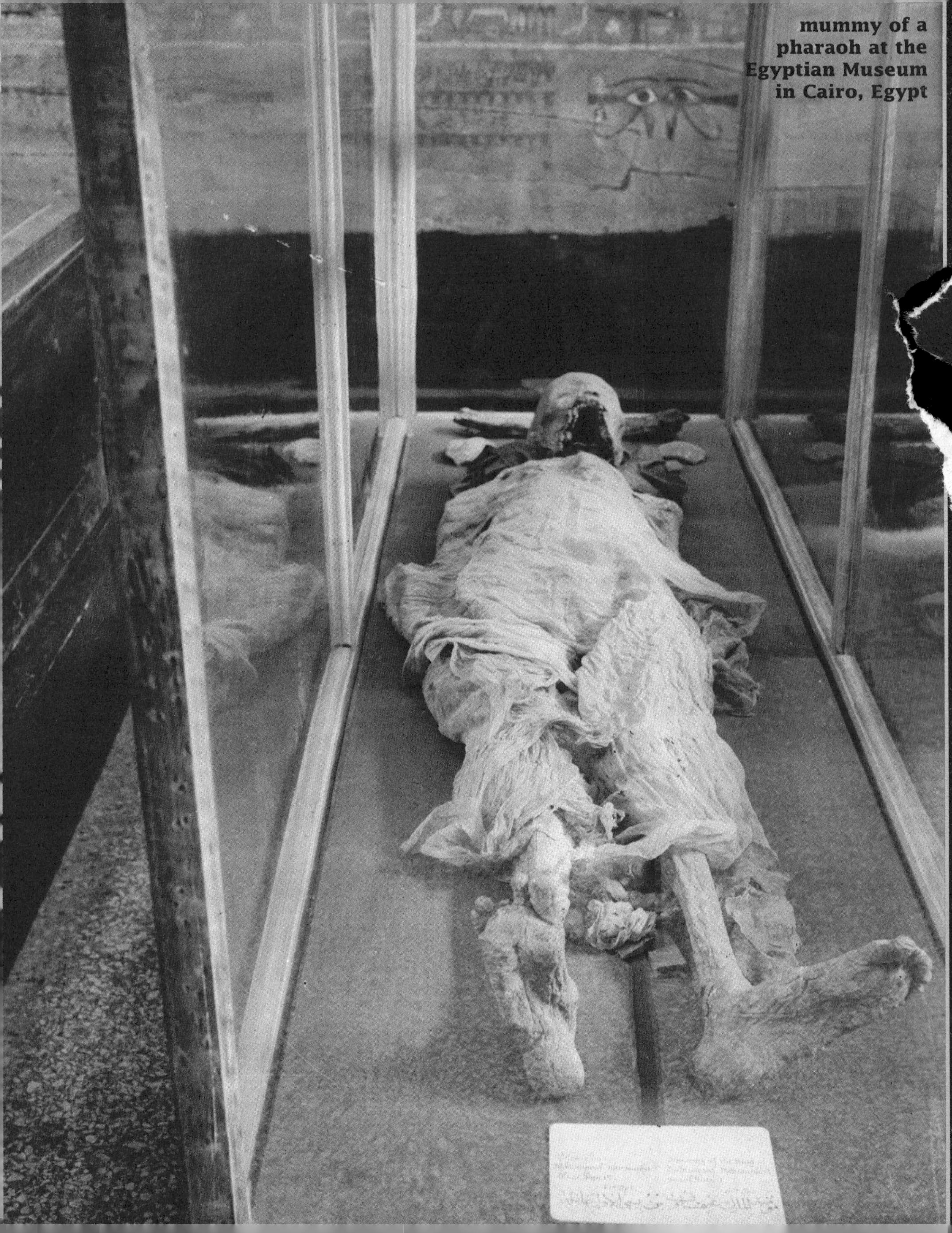

mummy of a pharaoh at the Egyptian Museum in Cairo, Egypt